NATIONAL GEOGRAPHIC

Ladders

NATIVE AMERICANS OF THE
SOUTHWEST

The Mystery of the Ancient Pueblo

by Sheri Reda

Late one afternoon on a fall day in 1888, two cowboys stumbled upon what looked like a tall city carved into the side of a cliff. The place was deserted. The only sounds were the whistling wind and the crunch of ice under their feet. Where were they?

The men had discovered the cliff dwellings of the ancient Pueblo at Mesa Verde. After its discovery, **archaeologists** rushed to the site to learn more about these people of long ago.

The ancient Pueblo began living in the Four Corners region—where Arizona, New Mexico, Colorado, and Utah meet— around A.D. 550. At first, they lived atop **mesas**, or hills with flat tops and steep sides. They hunted and gathered and made beautiful baskets.

Later generations of the ancient Pueblo mostly moved off the mesas. They settled in villages and grew corn, beans, and squash. They lived in pithouses, which are rooms built halfway underground with roofs made of sticks, stone, and clay. Later, they made homes using **adobe**, a mixture of clay and straw that they formed into bricks.

Around 1200, the ancient Pueblo started living in cliff dwellings. They moved to these high cliff dwellings, some archaeologists believe, as a response to enemy invaders. Then, only a hundred years later, they suddenly abandoned their cliff dwellings and moved to the southern part of the region. No one knows why.

Descendants of the ancient Pueblo, including the Hopi and Zuni people, still live in this region of the American Southwest today. Even they aren't sure why their ancestors left the Four Corners area.

∧ This is Cliff Palace, the largest cliff dwelling at Mesa Verde. Mesa Verde is one of the best-preserved sites of the ancient Pueblo.

∨ Some of these petroglyphs depict legends, or traditional stories that may or may not be historically true. This one shows Kokopelli. He is a popular mythical figure in Southwest culture.

Messages from Long Ago

We study ancient people by looking at they way they lived—from the style of their homes to the pictures they drew.

The art of the ancient Pueblo provides us with clues about their beliefs, their struggles, and their daily lives. Some of their art depicts people hunting animals. Other art pieces, like the picture at left, may depict a legend or a prediction about the future. But these are only educated guesses. Just like the ancient Pueblo themselves, many of the symbols in their art remain a mystery to us.

The ancient Pueblo made art using the materials around them. They made yellow, green, and red paints from nearby plants. Like many traditional peoples throughout the world, the ancient Pueblo painted handprints on rock. They also used sharp stones to create **petroglyphs**, or rock carvings. The best rocks to carve petroglyphs on were dark on the outside with lighter colored rock inside. As the artist carved away the dark surface, the lighter rock was revealed.

Even though a lot of rock art survives over many years, this beautiful artwork can be very delicate and easily damaged by humans. People visiting these rock art sites need to be especially careful not to damage the art. The artwork of the ancient Pueblo still holds many secrets. Archaeologists are uncovering these secrets by working with the modern Pueblo to decipher the meaning of the art.

Household Pottery

Pottery also provides clues about the lives of the ancient Pueblo. Many types of pottery have been discovered in the cliff dwellings. The people who lived there left behind pots, dishes, and even clay figures inside rooms protected from wind, rain, and snow. These ancient pots and dishes are in amazingly good shape, considering their age. They look like they've been sitting around for seven days instead of 700 years.

What's so great about old dishes and pots? They tell us about the everyday lives of the people who used them. For example, some pots are decorated with designs from tribes living in other places. The foreign designs tell us the ancient Pueblo were traders who exchanged goods with people from different regions.

Archaeologists also study the ways that the ancient Pueblo's household items were made.

The materials they used to make pottery tell us about the resources that were available to them. We know the ancient Pueblo had mud to make clay, because of their many clay pots and bowls.

Pieces of very old pottery are scattered all over ancient Pueblo ruins. These broken pieces provide more clues. For example, different colors and patterns come from different time periods. They make it possible to tell when the pottery was made and used.

< Ancient Pueblo artists made this pottery figure sometime between A.D. 900 and 1200.

6

Most pottery was used for everyday activities, such as cooking or carrying water. Special pieces were used during ceremonies.

Empty Houses

So why did the ancient Pueblo leave their cliff dwellings? We know they left what is now Colorado and Utah in about 1300, barely a century after they began living there. They migrated south into Arizona, New Mexico, and Mexico, where many of their descendants, such as the Hopi and Zuni, still live today.

Archaeologists have a few theories about why the ancient Pueblo left. One theory is that drought, or a period of no rain, made it impossible for them to farm and feed themselves. Another theory suggests that war overwhelmed the struggling civilization. Or perhaps the groups living together had many disagreements that led them all to seek a more peaceful place to live.

Descendants of the ancient Pueblo, including the Hopi and the Zuni, still live in adobe houses. Some modern Pueblo live on top of mesas, while others live in modern communities. They work with scientists and the government to protect artifacts and heritage sites. They want people to be able to learn about their culture for years to come. In time, they may also find out for sure why the ancient Pueblo abandoned their cliff dwellings.

∧ Some elements of ancient Pueblo culture live on in the dance, language, and art of modern Pueblo (shown here). They use bright colors and graphic patterns in their art and clothing.

∨ This deserted landscape in Utah was once home to a community of ancient Pueblo. Below is a group of stones that formed the round base of a kiva. A kiva is a building used for gatherings and ceremonies.

Check In What do pottery artifacts tell us about the lives of the ancient Pueblo?

Rise of the Navajo Code Talkers

by Sheri Reda

illustrated by Owen Brozman

It was December of 1941, and World War II was raging. The United States had stayed out of the war until the Japanese bombed Hawaii's Pearl Harbor. The United States then declared war. Early battles did not go well. The Japanese were breaking the codes the U.S. military used to send messages and instructions to their soldiers. The United States had to find a better way to send top secret messages to soldiers in the field. Otherwise, the enemy would continue to uncover their plans.

THERE WERE NO NAVAJO WORDS FOR MILITARY PLANES AND SHIPS. SO NAVAJO SOLDIERS INVENTED TERMS FOR MILITARY EQUIPMENT. DURING TRAINING, RECRUITS LEARNED MORE THAN 200 WORDS AND PHRASES FOR THE CODE.

WE NEED A NAVAJO WORD FOR "DIVE BOMBER." HOW ABOUT "CHICKEN HAWK"?

GREAT IDEA! IN NAVAJO, "CHICKEN HAWK" IS "GINI." THAT'LL BE THE CODE WORD FOR "DIVE BOMBER."

THEY KEPT TRACK OF ALL THE NEW TERMS THEY'D INVENTED.

MILITARY CRAFT	NAVAJO WORD	MEANING OF NAVAJO WORD IN ENGLISH
Dive Bomber	Gini	Chicken Hawk
Torpedo Plane	Tas-chizzie	Swallow
Observation Plane	Ne-ahs-jah	Owl
Fighter Plane	Da-he-tih-hi	Hummingbird
Bomber Plane	Jav-sho	Buzzard
Transport Plane	Astah	Eagle
Battleship	Lo-tso	Whale
Aircraft Carrier	Tsidi-ney-ye-hi	Bird carrier
Submarine	Besh-lo	Iron fish

English Letter	English Word	Navajo Word
A	ANT	WOL-LA-CHEE
A	APPLE	BE-LA-SANA
A	AXE	TSE-NILL
B	BADGER	NA-HASH-CHID
B	BEAR	SHUSH
B	BARREL	TOISH-JEH
C	CAT	MOASI
C	COAL	TLA-GIN
C	COW	BA-GOSHI
D	DEER	BE
D	DEVIL	CHINDI
D	DOG	LHA-CHA-EH
E	EAR	AH-JAH
E	ELK	DZEH
E	EYE	AH-NAH

TO USE WORDS THAT WEREN'T IN THE LIST FOR MILITARY EQUIPMENT, THEY SPELLED OUT THOSE WORDS IN CODE. THEY USED NAVAJO WORDS FOR LETTERS IN THE ENGLISH ALPHABET. USING THE CHART ABOVE, WHAT ARE TWO WAYS OF SPELLING THE WORD "BEE" USING THE CODE?

AMERICA HONORS [THE] NATIVE AMERICANS WHO . . . GAVE THEIR COUNTRY A SERVICE ONLY THEY COULD GIVE. IN WAR, USING THEIR NATIVE LANGUAGE, THEY RELAYED SECRET MESSAGES THAT TURNED THE COURSE OF BATTLE . . . TODAY, WE GIVE THESE EXCEPTIONAL MARINES THE RECOGNITION THEY EARNED LONG AGO.

THEN, IN 2001, PRESIDENT GEORGE W. BUSH PRESENTED CONGRESSIONAL GOLD MEDALS TO THE FOUR SURVIVING ORIGINAL CODE TALKERS. HE PRESENTED SILVER MEDALS TO THE DOZENS OF LIVING CODE TALKERS WHO CAME AFTER THIS GROUP.

MANY OF THE CODE TALKERS DID NOT LIVE LONG ENOUGH TO RECEIVE THESE HONORS.

CHESTER NEZ, THE LAST SURVIVING MEMBER OF THE ORIGINAL NAVAJO CODE TALKERS, GAVE A SPEECH IN 2013 ABOUT HIS EXPERIENCES IN THE WAR. HIS ROLE WAS SO IMPORTANT THAT HE AND THE OTHER CODE TALKERS WERE ALWAYS ON DUTY IN CASE A MESSAGE CAME THROUGH.

TOGETHER, THE ORIGINAL CODE TALKERS CREATED THE ONLY UNBROKEN CODE IN MODERN MILITARY HISTORY.

Check In How did the Navajo Code Talkers make a contribution to the war effort and serve their country?

ANIMAL SYMBOLISM
in the Southwest

by Brett Gover

HOPI WOVEN PLAQUE BASKET

> Turtle

In many southwestern Native American cultures, the turtle is a symbol of Earth. They both move slowly and steadily. Can you find the turtle on this woven basket?

Animals play a big role in the culture, religion, and **mythology** of Native Americans of the Southwest. Many stories and myths tell about animals with human qualities. They can speak, get angry, and learn from mistakes. Sometimes the animals even have **divine** qualities, such as the ability to change the weather. But the stories also play up an animal's natural strengths or weaknesses, and teach lessons about life through their adventures.

ZUNI TERRA-COTTA OWL

Because of their great respect for animals, Native Americans incorporate animal **symbols** into pottery designs, carvings, jewelry, sand paintings, and other types of art. These symbols do not just represent the animal itself. They also represent the specific traits or qualities associated with that animal.

∧ Owl

Owls can see in the dark. They can spot tiny animals at a great distance. The owl represents wisdom, truth, and the ability to see things that others cannot. They are protectors of the home.

∨ Frog

Frogs represent water, rain, and fertility. Frogs live both in water (when they are tadpoles) and on land. When tadpoles and frogs appear together in Native American artwork, they represent the cycle of life.

ZUNI PUEBLO WATER CARRIER

The Protector

If you met a bear, you might be filled with fear. After all, they are large, intimidating animals. To the Zuni people of New Mexico, however, the bear is an important symbol of protection. In fact, some think that if you "feed" a tiny bear carving by putting a little cornmeal in front of it, the bear will guard your home while you are gone.

ZUNI BEAR FETISH

The heartline carved into the side of this bear fetish shows the movement the animal's breath takes from its mouth toward its heart or soul.

The bear carving is called a fetish. A fetish is a small object that people believe has special powers or symbolic meaning. The Zuni create fetishes of animals that are important to them. They believe these animals and the fetishes that represent them have special healing powers. It is common for fetishes to have straight or zigzagging arrows called heartlines. A heartline shows the path of the animal's breath. The Zuni believe that the heartline gives the fetish much of its healing powers.

To the Zuni, bears represent qualities such as instinct and strength. They also represent the ability to adapt to change. The bear inspires courage to look within and to face problems in life.

> The Zuni world was made up of six important directions. Each direction had its own color and guardian. The bear was the guardian of the west. The color for the west was blue, possibly for the blue of the ocean.

The Guardian

An eagle can soar in the sky and still hunt for prey far below. Its eyesight is incredible. Even from a great height, it can spot a gopher scurrying to its burrow or a fish surfacing in a stream. This bird of prey has eyes that are nearly as large as human eyes, and its vision is much sharper than ours. A combination of huge wings, powerful claws, and keen eyesight makes eagles fearsome hunters.

In the traditions of southwestern Native Americans, the eagle is the guardian of the Upper Region, one of the six sacred directions. These include the four directions we know (north, south, east, and west), plus one overhead and one under the ground. In this role, the eagle serves as messenger to the gods, carrying people's prayers to them. The eagle symbolizes courage, wisdom, strength, and dignity. Some Native American peoples greatly value eagle feathers and use them in sacred ceremonies.

ANCIENT EAGLE PENDANT

∧ To the Zuni, the eagle is the guardian of the sky. The Zuni consider the eagle to be the younger brother of the wolf, who is guardian of the east.

> This woven basket shows an image of an eagle. Many Native Americans use this kind of basket as a bowl.

HOPI WICKER BASKET

Have you ever wondered how the bald eagle got its name? After all, its head is not bald. The answer is that the word *bald* once meant "white."

The Healer

Lizards are some of the most common animals in the Southwest. Some are no bigger than your little finger. Others are as long as your arm. There are dozens of different kinds of lizards living in this region. It isn't surprising that lizard designs are so common in the artwork of southwestern Native Americans.

The Gila monster is one of them. This fork-tongued, two-foot-long creature spends most of its life underground in its burrow. It is one of only two poisonous lizards in the world. But even though its poison is harmful to humans, the Gila monster often represents preservation and survival in the mythology of southwestern Native Americans. In many legends, the Gila monster is the hero.

The curious-looking lizard also symbolizes health, prosperity, protection, and happiness. Some people believe the Gila monster's scaly skin has the power to heal. Scientists have recently discovered that this lizard's venom might be useful in fighting diseases such as diabetes.

O'ODHAM BASKET

> Lizards decorate this basket. It was made long ago by the O'odham people in what is now south-central Arizona.

∨ Some lizards are brightly colored, while some are rather dull. The Gila monster's scales warn other animals to stay away.

Check In Describe some of the characteristics that these animals symbolize to the southwestern Native Americans.

How Coyote Stole the Sun

by Elizabeth Massie   illustrated by Richard Downs

Cultures all around the world tell folk tales. Many of these stories attempt to explain why or how something in nature came to be, such as why grass is green or why spiders have eight legs. This type of folk tale is called a *pourquoi* (poor-KWA) tale because pourquoi means "why" in French. The following Zuni story, which tells how winter came to be, features Coyote, a popular trickster in many Native American stories.

Many years ago, all the land was dark. Though the weather was always warm, there was no light. Many animals struggled to survive in the unending darkness, especially Coyote. He could not see where he was going, which made it almost impossible to hunt.

Coyote was jealous of Eagle, who had sharp eyesight and could see in the darkness. One day, Coyote called up to Eagle, who sat perched on a boulder with a big, fat snake in her sharp talons.

"Hey, Eagle," he said, "I wish I could hunt as well as you, but it is just too dark and my eyes can't find the prey I need to catch."

Eagle tipped her head, thinking, and then replied, "I know where there is light, and I can take you there if you'd like."

"I'd like that," said Coyote. "Don't race too far ahead, or I'll lose sight of you."

After feeding the snake to her noisy eaglets, Eagle flew off westward with Coyote running after her. They traveled over flat stretches of desert, rocky riverbeds, and high, craggy hills.

Coyote stubbed his toe on a rock and shouted, "Ow! Slow down!"

"Why don't you watch where you're going?" called Eagle.

It was so dark, Coyote couldn't see where he was going, but when he told Eagle this, Eagle just sighed and kept on flying.

Finally, the two reached the dark, outer parts of a village. In the center of the village, people were dancing and singing around a mysterious glowing box.

Coyote and Eagle sat in the shadows, watching. Coyote blinked and squinted because he was not used to seeing light. He whispered to Eagle, "Let's steal the light and take it back with us!"

Eagle shook her feathery head and said, "That would be unfair, but we could ask to borrow it for a while."

Coyote snorted, rolled his eyes, and pointed to the dancers. "Just look at them. They enjoy the light far too much to let us borrow it. Please, Eagle, let's steal it, for they have had it long enough and now it's our turn!"

Eagle hesitated at first, but she finally swooped down and snatched the box of light with her talons. She flew away with Coyote racing along behind her.

As they hurried back toward the east, Coyote noticed how easy it was to see his way now. He started to become very curious about the box of light. He wanted to peek inside, but as long as Eagle had it in her talons, he couldn't get near it.

"Eagle," he called, "let me carry the box for a while. Without the weight of that box, it will be much easier for you to fly."

Eagle replied, "No, thank you."

Coyote thought that Eagle might change her mind. Again he hollered, "Eagle, give me the box to carry, for then you can fly freely!"

Eagle was growing irritated, but she replied politely, "No, thank you."

Much later, Coyote cried, "Come on, Eagle, give me the box to carry. Please, please, please!"

Weary of the requests, Eagle at last agreed. She flew to the ground and handed the box to Coyote, but then she looked him in the eye and gave him a stern warning. "Do not open the box, for it is meant to stay shut. Just its glow is enough to let you see in the darkness."

"I won't open it," promised Coyote, though he was itching to see inside.

Eagle flew on ahead, leaving Coyote alone with the box of light.

29

For a short while, Coyote carried the box across the desert, but his curiosity finally got the best of him. He stopped, put the box down, and looked at it carefully. He walked around it, touching it with his paw, sniffing it, and even licking the side of the box to see if light might have a special taste, but none of this satisfied him.

"Enough of this," Coyote said to himself. "What harm can one quick look do?"

With that, Coyote flipped off the top of the box with his long nose.

Suddenly there was a loud *whoosh!* and Coyote was knocked backward as the sun and moon, which had been closed tight inside the box, flew up into the sky.

As the bright sun flew higher and higher into the sky, farther and farther away, the weather became very cold, and it began to snow. The snow grew deeper and deeper. Coyote shivered and looked around, hoping no other creature had seen what he had done.

But Eagle, with her powerful eyes, had seen, and she flew back to where Coyote sat covered in snow.

"I should never have given in to your begging," she said. "You have let out the light and warmth of the sun, but now it is so far away that you've also brought cold weather to the world!"

Coyote hung his head in shame. Yes, he had brought light to the world, but by letting the light escape, he had also created winter.

Check In Describe the characters of Coyote and Eagle. How did their personalities affect their actions in the story?

Discuss

1. What connects the four selections you read in this book? What makes you think that?

2. Based on the evidence presented in the first selection, what do you think happened to the ancient Pueblo people?

3. How did the U. S. military and the Navajo work together during World War II? What were some of the challenges of using Navajo as the basis for a code?

4. What life lessons can we learn from Coyote's actions in the folk tale?

5. Which aspect of southwestern Native American culture do you want to learn more about? Why?